Table of Contents

CHAPTER 1

Stars and Planets

Look up into the sky at night. What do you see? **Stars**! Stars are huge balls of hot and glowing gases. They're so hot and so bright that you can see them from Earth even though they are very, very far away.

the Big Dipper

Most of these stars have **planets** around them. A planet is a large, round object that **orbits**, or travels around, a star. There are other rocks and objects that also orbit the Sun. But planets are special. They are larger and more round than other space objects.

planets orbiting a star

SMART WORDS

orbit: to travel around an object, like a star or planet

planet: a large, round object that orbits a star

star: a huge ball of very hot and glowing gases

Our Sun

What bright object can be found in the sky during the day? The **Sun**! Did you know that the Sun is a star? Earth is one of the planets that orbits our Sun. Can you think of another planet?

the Sun in the sky

The Sun is at the very center of our **solar system**. In fact, solar means sun.

Everything in our solar system orbits the Sun.

Some planets go around quickly. Others are slower.

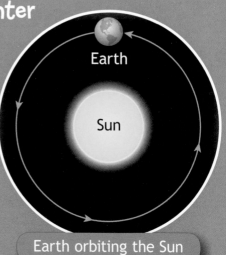

Earth

Sun

Earth orbiting the Sun

The time it takes for a planet to orbit the Sun is the length of that planet's year. Earth takes 365 days to orbit the Sun. That's why Earth's year is 365 days.

SMART WORDS

Sun: the star that Earth and other planets orbit that gives us light and warmth

solar system: the Sun, the eight planets, and other objects that orbit the Sun

5

Our Solar System

Our solar system has eight planets. Some planets are made of rock. Others are made of gas. Planets like Venus are very hot — too hot to live on. Others like Neptune are very cold. One planet is not too hot or too cold. Can you guess which planet is just right? Earth!

our solar system

Sun

Mercury

Venus

Eart

There's an easy way to remember the names of the planets and their order from the Sun. Here's the trick: Just look at the first letter of each of the words in this saying:

My Very Educated Mother Just Served Us Nachos

Mercury
Venus
Earth
Mars
Jupiter
Saturn
Uranus
Neptune

rs

Jupiter

Saturn

Uranus

Neptune

USE YOUR SMART WORDS

On a piece of paper, draw the solar system. Label your drawing with your Smart Words.

orbit   planet   solar system   star   Sun

our solar system

Neptune

Sun

Jupiter

Saturn

Earth

Uranus

Mercury

Venus   Mars

TALK LIKE A SCIENTIST

Imagine you are a teacher. What trick can you give your students to help them remember the names of all the planets in our solar system?

MAKE A SOLAR SYSTEM MOBILE!

You will need:

- black paper plate
- star stickers
- hole punch
- paper
- scissors
- string
- tape

1. Use the star stickers to decorate a paper plate so it looks like a starry night sky.

2. Punch nine holes in the paper plate: one in the center for the Sun and eight more for the planets.

3. Draw nine circles on paper. Use the picture on page 8 to help you make different sizes for the Sun and each planet.

4. Color the circles to match the Sun and each planet.

5. Cut out the circles and punch a hole at the top of each one.

6. Cut nine pieces of string and attach them to the holes in the circles. Attach the other ends of the strings to the holes in the paper plate. Use tape to hold the strings in place.

7. Tape a longer string to the center of the paper plate. Now find a good spot to hang your solar system mobile!

CHAPTER 2

Rocky Planets

There are four rocky planets. Mercury is one of them. It is the smallest planet in our solar system. It is about the same size as Earth's moon. It orbits the Sun very fast. One year on Mercury is only 88 days. If you lived on Mercury, you would celebrate your birthday four times a year!

MERCURY

Surface: Rocky
Length of Day: 59 Earth Days
Length of Year: 88 Earth Days
Number of Moons: 0

Mercury compared to Earth

Mercury   Earth

Mercury is the closest planet to the Sun. During the day, it is ten times hotter than the hottest summer day on Earth. But the nights are colder than the inside of a freezer. Brrrr!

Mercury is covered in big holes called **craters**. It has more craters than any other planet. The craters were made when huge space rocks smashed into it.

Mercury's craters

SMART WORD

crater: a large, bowl-shaped hole on a moon or planet usually caused by a crashing space rock

Venus

Do you know any twins? Venus is often called Earth's twin. It's about the same size as Earth. It's also our closest planet neighbor. But that is where the similarities stop. You could never live on Venus.

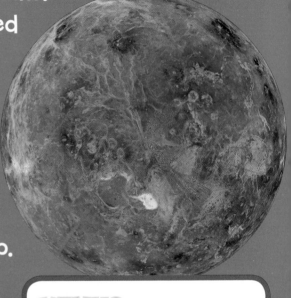

VENUS
Surface: Rocky
Length of Day: 243 Earth Days
Length of Year: 224 Earth Days
Number of Moons: 0

Venus compared to Earth

Venus   Earth

Venus is the second planet from the Sun. It is the hottest planet in our solar system. It's so hot, it sizzles! Venus has thick yellow clouds that trap heat from the Sun.

The surface of Venus is covered in **volcanoes**. These volcanoes have erupted all over the planet, creating strange shapes. Some of these look like pancakes — but they are too hot to eat!

surface of Venus

SMART WORD

volcano: an opening in the surface of a planet from which gas and other material escapes

Earth

Planet Earth is our home. It is the third planet from the Sun. It's not too hot and not too cold. It's not too dry and not too wet. Some people call Earth the Goldilocks planet. Can you guess why? It's just right for things to live and grow!

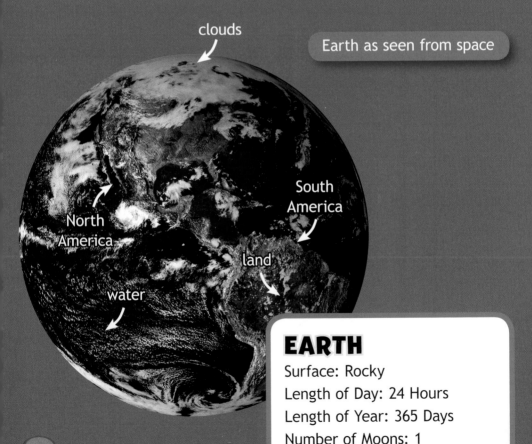

clouds

Earth as seen from space

North America

South America

land

water

EARTH
Surface: Rocky
Length of Day: 24 Hours
Length of Year: 365 Days
Number of Moons: 1

Earth is very special. It's the only planet —
that we know of — that has life. Plants and
animals live everywhere on Earth. They live
on land and in water.

Most of Earth is covered with water. That's
why it looks so blue from outer space!

one of Earth's oceans

Our Moon

Our solar system has just one star but many **moons**. Like a planet, a moon is round and travels in an orbit. But instead of orbiting the Sun, a moon orbits a planet. Some planets have many moons. Some planets have no moons. The Earth is the only planet with just one moon.

Moon

the Earth and the Moon

Earth

The Moon is our closest neighbor in space. But unlike Earth, there is no life on the Moon. There is no air to breathe or water to drink. There are no clouds or rain or wind or snow.

Earth's Moon is made of rocks. Like Mercury, it is covered in craters.

the Moon's craters

SMART WORD

moon: a round object made of rock or ice that orbits a planet

Mars

Of all the planets, Mars is most like Earth. Both are made of rocks. Like Earth, Mars has many mountains and volcanoes. Earth has one moon. But Mars has two.

MARS
Surface: Rocky
Length of Day: 25 hours
Length of Year: 687 Earth Days
Number of Moons: 2

Mars compared to Earth

Mars

Earth

Mars is also very different from Earth. Earth looks like a big blue ball. Mars is a deep red color. It is called the Red Planet because its rocks are full of rusty iron.

There is no air to breathe on Mars, and it is very cold. It has strong winds that blow its soil around. These dust storms can last for months.

the red and dusty surface of Mars

USE YOUR

SMART WORDS

Fill in each blank with a Smart Word.

craters   volcanoes   Moon

The Moon has many holes called _____.

The _____ is our closest neighbor in space.

The surface of Venus is covered in fiery _____.

TALK LIKE A SCIENTIST

Your class is taking the first ever trip to Mars. Come up with a list of things you need to take. Use your Smart Words to describe what you will find there.

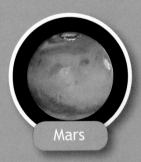

Mars

TRUE or FALSE?

Check the correct box to show which statements are true and which are false.

T F

☐ ☐ Mercury is the smallest planet in our solar system.

☐ ☐ The surface of Mercury is covered in craters.

☐ ☐ Mars is known as Earth's twin.

☐ ☐ Earth is called the Goldilocks planet.

☐ ☐ Earth is the fourth planet from the Sun.

☐ ☐ The Moon has many craters.

☐ ☐ There is lots of water on the Moon.

☐ ☐ The weather on Mars is like Earth's.

☐ ☐ Venus is the hottest planet in our solar system.

☐ ☐ Mars has one moon.

CHAPTER 3

The Gas Planets

Some planets, like Earth, are made of rock. Others, like Jupiter, are made of **gas**. Gas is like air. Gas planets are huge balls of super thick air without a hard surface. What keeps Jupiter's gas from floating away and holds it in a round, planet-like shape? **Gravity**! Gravity is an invisible force that pulls the gas in.

JUPITER

Surface: Gas
Length of Day: 10 Hours
Length of Year: 12 Earth Years
Number of Moons: 67

Jupiter compared to Earth

Jupiter   Earth

Jupiter is the largest planet in our solar system. Over a thousand Earths could fit inside Jupiter!

Jupiter has 67 moons — more than any other planet. Its largest moon is three times the size of Earth's Moon and almost as big as Mars!

Ganymede

Ganymede is Jupiter's largest moon.

SMART WORDS

gas: a substance, like air, that does not have a hard surface

gravity: the force that pulls objects in space together and keeps them from floating away

Saturn

Saturn is the sixth planet from the Sun. It is the second largest planet — nine times larger than Earth. But it is so light that it would float in water! Like Jupiter, Saturn is made up mainly of gas.

SATURN
Surface: Gas
Length of Day: 11 Hours
Length of Year: 29 Earth Years
Number of Moons: 62

Saturn compared to Earth

Saturn   Earth

But what makes Saturn stand out from the rest? Its jumbo **rings**. The rings are made of bits of ice, rock, and dust. They look like hula hoops!

Saturn's rings

Saturn has 62 moons. Titan is the biggest. It's larger than Mercury! Just like Earth, Titan has oceans and lakes. But they are filled with poisonous liquids.

Titan

One year on Saturn is about 29 years on Earth. If you were born in 2008, your next birthday on Saturn wouldn't be until the year 2037!

SMART WORD

ring: a round hoop around a planet made of ice, rocks, and dust

Uranus

Next to Saturn is Uranus. It is also a gas planet. It is the third largest planet and four times the size of Earth. Uranus is the coldest planet in our solar system and appears as an icy blue color.

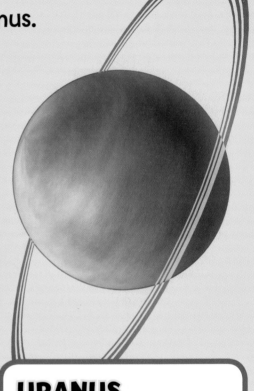

Uranus compared to Earth

Uranus   Earth

URANUS

Surface: Gas
Length of Day: 17 Hours
Length of Year: 84 Earth Years
Number of Moons: 27

What else is different about Uranus? It's sideways! Uranus is the only planet to spin on its side. This means that night on some parts of Uranus can last more than 40 years!

Like Saturn, Uranus has rings. But there are not as many, and they are not as bright.

Uranus has 27 moons. Its largest is Titania. Even so, Earth's Moon is about twenty times larger.

Titania

Neptune

Neptune is the eighth planet in our solar system. It is the farthest from the Sun. Neptune is about the same size as Uranus. Like Uranus, it is blue and made of gas. Neptune is the windiest planet in the solar system. The wind is so strong that it could pick up an elephant!

NEPTUNE

Surface: Gas
Length of Day: 16 Hours
Length of Year: 165 Earth Years
Number of Moons: 13

Neptune compared to Earth

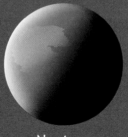
Neptune

Earth

Dwarf Planets

Dwarf planets are round objects like planets. They orbit the Sun just like other planets. But they are much smaller than the other planets in our solar system.

We know of five dwarf planets in our solar system. Scientists believe there are hundreds more!

Pluto is the most famous dwarf planet. It was named by an eleven-year-old girl! It used to be the ninth planet in our solar system. But scientists decided it was too small.

Pluto

SMART WORD

dwarf planet: a round object that is much smaller than a planet

USE YOUR SMART WORDS

Fill in each blank with a Smart Word.

dwarf planet   gas   gravity   rings

Planets and moons are held in their orbit by a force called _____.

_____ is a light substance like air that does not have a hard surface.

Saturn's _____ look just like hula hoops. They are made of ice, rock, and dust.

Pluto is the most famous _____.

TALK LIKE A SCIENTIST

A classmate says she wants to travel to Jupiter to see its great red spot. Explain why her space ship won't be able to land on Jupiter's surface. Use your Smart Words.

30

SMART WORDS GLOSSARY

crater: a large, bowl-shaped hole on a moon or planet usually caused by a crashing space rock

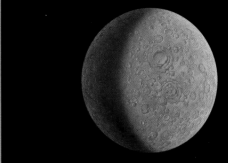

dwarf planet: a round object that is much smaller than a planet

gas: a substance, like air, that does not have a hard surface

gravity: the force that pulls objects in space together and keeps them from floating away

moon: a round object made of rock or ice that orbits a planet

orbit: to travel around an object, like a star or planet

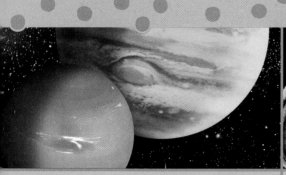

planet: a large, round object that orbits a star

rings: round hoops around a planet made of ice, rocks, and dust

solar system: the Sun, the eight planets, and other objects that orbit the Sun

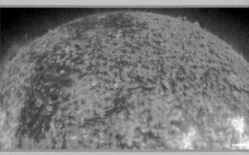

star: a huge ball of very hot and glowing gases

Sun: the star that Earth and other planets orbit that gives us light and warmth

volcano: an opening in the surface of a planet from which gas and other material escapes

USE YOUR SMART WORDS ANSWERS

PAGE 20: craters, Moon, volcanoes

PAGE 21: T, T, F, T, F, T, F, F, T, F

PAGE 30: gravity, gas, rings, dwarf planet